TO: ....

FROM: ....

D1611329

Published by Sourcebooks Casablanca, an imprint of Sourcebooks, Inc.
P.O. Box 4410, Naperville, Illinois 60567-4410
(630) 961-3900
Fax: (630) 961-2168
www.sourcebooks.com

Printed and bound in the United States of America.
SP 10 9 8 7 6 5 4 3 2 1

REDEEM THIS COUPON FOR A

slow, sexy striptease—

FOR YOUR EYES ONLY.

Steamy.

IT'S GETTING HOT IN HERE.
HAND OVER THIS COUPON AND
let's take off all our clothes.

**PRESENT THIS COUPON AND
I'LL FULFILL YOUR**

hottest fantasy.

**JUST WHISPER IT IN MY EAR,
AND I'LL MAKE IT HAPPEN.**

Steamy.

**YOU. ME.
AND A HOT SHOWER TOGETHER.
HAND OVER THIS COUPON AND**

let the steam rise!

**TURN IN THIS COUPON
FOR A PASSIONATE,**

drop-everything quickie.

Steamy.

THIS COUPON IS GOOD FOR SOME

steamy erotica.

I'LL READ WHILE YOU LISTEN.

Steamy

LET ME COOL YOU OFF RIGHT.
PRESENT THIS COUPON AND

I'll tantalize you

WITH AN ICE CUBE IN WAYS
YOU WON'T BELIEVE.

PRESENT THIS COUPON AND

I'll undress you—

USING ONLY MY TEETH.

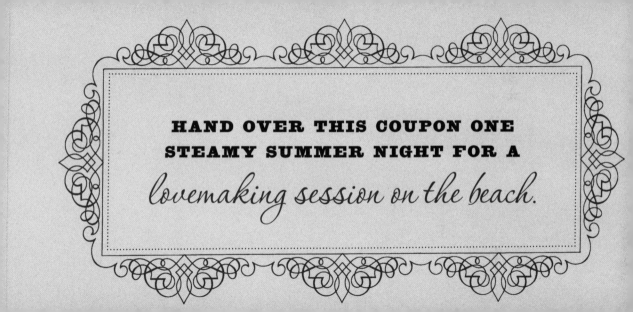

HAND OVER THIS COUPON ONE STEAMY SUMMER NIGHT FOR A

lovemaking session on the beach.

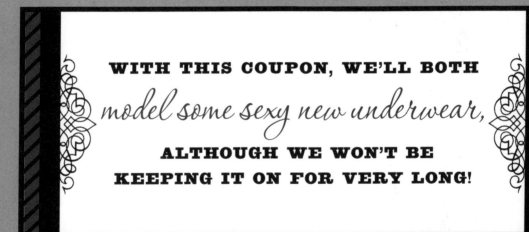

WITH THIS COUPON, WE'LL BOTH

model some sexy new underwear,

ALTHOUGH WE WON'T BE
KEEPING IT ON FOR VERY LONG!

Steamy.

PRESENT THIS COUPON WHEN

you want to be teased.

**JUST WATCH ME UNTIL
YOU CAN'T WAIT ANY LONGER.**

THIS COUPON IS GOOD FOR A

wild romp

IN A HOT TUB OR SAUNA—YOU PICK.

Steamy.

REDEEM FOR SOME

hot makeup sex.

**WHAT BETTER WAY TO COOL DOWN
AFTER FEELING STEAMED?**

HAND OVER THIS COUPON TO

feel my hot tongue

**EXPLORE YOUR MOST
SENSITIVE AREAS.**

Steamy

WITH THIS COUPON, WE'LL

make love in every room

OF THE HOUSE OVER THE NEXT WEEK.

HAND OVER THIS COUPON FOR A

delicious lovemaking session.

I'LL BRING THE WHIPPED CREAM.

Steamy.

**REDEEM THIS COUPON
AND WE'LL TRY A**

new position—

YOU DECIDE WHICH ONE.

**HAND OVER THIS
COUPON TO SEE ME**

naked and lying on the bed

FOR AS LONG AS YOU WISH.

**PRESENT THIS COUPON
WHEN YOU WANT TO BE SEDUCED.
YOU WON'T BELIEVE**

how tempting I can be.

Want to see something hot?

**REDEEM THIS COUPON AND WE'LL
WATCH A DIRTY MOVIE OR LOOK AT
NAUGHTY PICTURES TOGETHER.**

Steamy.

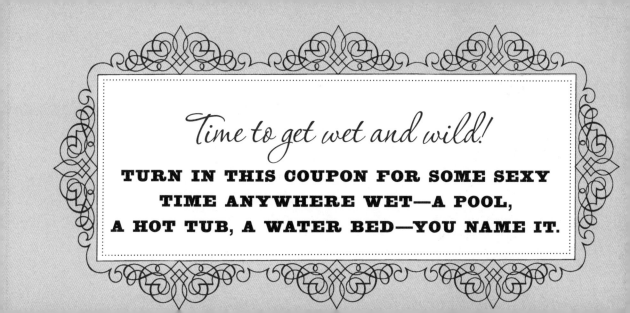

Time to get wet and wild!

**TURN IN THIS COUPON FOR SOME SEXY
TIME ANYWHERE WET—A POOL,
A HOT TUB, A WATER BED—YOU NAME IT.**

THERE ARE LOTS OF WAYS TO KISS.
HAND OVER THIS COUPON AND

I'll kiss you anywhere—

AND IN ANY WAY—YOU CHOOSE.